The Grammar Graduate's Parts of Speech

Laurie Boyd

ISBN 978-0-9969221-2-8

A FAVORITE CHILD PRESS

Kansas City, Kansas

laurieboyd@laurieboyd.com

www.thegrammargraduate.com

Parts of Speech

Contents:

How to Use This Material

Why Learn the Parts of Speech

Familiarity with the eight parts of speech – what they are, and how each one functions in a sentence – may seem like unimportant trivia, but this is foundational knowledge for learning to speak and write Academic English.

Many post-high school opportunities and higher-paying jobs or careers depend on an individual's ability to speak and write fluently according to the rules of Academic English. For this reason, many people call Academic English the "green" language or the "cash" register.

Tests in school, including college, are written in Academic English. Teachers and professors expect students to speak and write fluently in Academic English. Many intelligent young people struggle in higher education simply because they are not fully fluent with this standard.

Here are just a few of the rules you must understand in order to become adept at using Academic English:

- subject-verb agreement
- pronoun-antecedent agreement
- punctuation and capitalization
- subordination of ideas
- parallel construction

It is nearly impossible to learn these conventions if you do not learn the terminology and understand the concepts of the parts of speech.

You have to be able to recognize parts of speech in order to understand how to identify phrases and clauses. You have to understand phrases and clauses in order to apply spelling and usage rules and to fix sentence errors like fragments and run-ons. You have to use several kinds of sentence structures in order for your writing to sound intelligent and sophisticated.

Teachers of foreign languages often bemoan the fact that they have to teach English grammar to English-speaking students before they can teach them the grammatical structure of a second language. This product provides just enough exposure to, and practice with, the parts of speech to prepare individuals to learn a foreign language.

The good news is, you already understand a lot of these concepts because you have learned a language. You have considerable expertise already. These lessons provide labels for the concepts you already intuit and use every day.

Learning how language works is fascinating. Words carry meaning, and our use of words can be rich, creative, humorous, and moving. People groups from different countries, or even different regions within the same country, often speak different dialects, which is endlessly interesting.

Those dialects, however, can present challenges to students who are trying to learn and use Academic English, because the rules of Academic English may not sound as "correct" or as acceptable as one's spoken dialect. Once non-Academic English speakers learn the conventions of Academic English, they will find themselves code-switching between their cultural use of language and that of Academic English, depending on their audience.

Bias and prejudice based on an individual's use of language, while judgmental and unfair, is common. Educators, employers, and co-workers may judge people who speak or write only non-Academic English as unintelligent, incorrect, or improper. I want my students to have every advantage possible for leveling the playing field as they seek higher education or employment.

For this reason, I have identified several non-Academic, dialectic structures that are common among the students who live in my region, whether they are black, brown, white, or other. In the lesson packets, these common usages are identified in bold letters in outlined boxes. They all start with "Please note," and they are tagged with the Grammar Graduate pencil cartoon, like this:

> **Please note that "theirselves" is not used in Academic English. Use "themselves".**

The last lesson in this resource reviews these few commonly used, non-Academic English structures and provides practice in converting them to Academic English.

The Note-Taker

The Note-Taker provides a chart in which to record the most basic information about each part of speech while you are learning. The Note-Taker in the Student's Pages is blank. The Note-Taker in the Teacher's Key is filled in for you. The Teacher's Key begins on page 85.

You may want to distribute the empty Note-Taker pages to your students and have them take notes as you introduce and "teach" each part of speech, using the copy in the Teacher's Key. If you don't have a teacher, you may use the completed Note-Taker from the Teacher's Key (pp. 87-88) to decide how to complete the blanks in each lesson packet. You can teach this material to yourself.

Lesson Packets

We provide a lesson packet for each part of speech (two lesson packets for Verbs). Each lesson begins with definitions and examples. Several practice exercises are included, one exercise following each small chunk of instruction throughout the lesson.

You will want to read every word of each packet since the information is already as abbreviated as we could make it and still include the necessary concepts. The teacher can use the Teacher's Key copies and just tell students how to fill in the blanks of the explanations as you read together, or the teacher may challenge the students to first try to make sense of the blanks by referring to the completed Note-Taker.

Be sure to study the lessons in order. Applications for certain parts of speech depend on knowledge about certain other parts of speech. For example, adjectives give more information about nouns; therefore, a student must be able to identify nouns before he or she will be able to work well with adjectives. Many of the same words used for prepositions also appear in sentences as adverbs, so some knowledge of adverbs is necessary before studying prepositions. The parts of speech are listed in the Note-Taker in the same recommended order as the lesson packets.

A teacher of middle school students, who is responsible for teaching many components of a Language Arts curriculum, may want to cover only one packet a week, reviewing concepts from day to day, ending the week with the quiz over a single part of speech. An individual studying for his or her own edification, however, can take himself through the lessons at his own pace and quiz himself along the way.

Quizzes

For all the parts of speech, except Interjections, we provide a quiz for assessing progress in learning the concepts. Most of these quizzes are only one page in length. These may be used however you wish, of course – as extra practice, as a graded assessment, or as a self-assessment. To cement learning, however, we recommend that learners work to understand any mistakes they make on the quizzes and study the lesson packet information further in order to correct their responses. Giving an "Open Note" quiz allows students to use their completed packets to figure out answers to any questions with which they struggle.

That being said, we know that we have included some levels of concepts that no one (other than a linguist or a grammar teacher) will need to know long-term. But studying the classifications of conjunctions, for example, deepens learners' familiarity with the way language is structured. Whether learners remember all of the details about each classification or not, they are more likely to recognize a word as a conjunction after studying all of the categories, even if they cannot recall which ones are coordinating, correlative, or subordinating.

Speaking of classifications of conjunctions, we provide a one-page quiz for each of the three major classifications of conjunctions, rather than one page over all of the conjunctions together. You may want to take each quiz after each section in the lesson packet on conjunctions rather than wait until the very end.

Interjections are so simple and easily recognizable that we did not write a quiz for this final part of speech in the sequence of lessons.

Comprehensive Review

The Comprehensive Review for the entire *Parts of Speech* book consists of several paragraphs. These exercises challenge the learner to identify literally every word in a paragraph as a single part of speech. Be sure to remind students throughout each lesson that any word's part of speech is determined by how it is used in a particular sentence, and students must learn to ask themselves certain questions for identifying the various parts of speech. We offer several paragraphs in our Comprehensive Review so that learners may practice this exercise several times.

Because this book does not cover infinitives and other verbals, none of our sentences for these exercises will include infinitives, gerunds, or participles. The Teacher's Key for the Comprehensive Review provides the answers to the exercises.

Opportunities for You and Your Students

As a purchaser, you have the right to reproduce (copy) these pages for your use in teaching and learning parts of speech. An easier option for a class is to purchase the book for every learner and use it as a consumable. This way your students have the lessons to carry with them as a reference to use in higher levels of their schooling.

Finally, you will want to join our community in order to learn about new products as they become available. Sign up for our free newsletter at www.thegrammargraduate.com, and get free resources in your e-mail inbox from time to time.

We sincerely hope this material is helpful in your endeavors to teach or learn Academic English.

Parts of Speech: Note-Taker

Name _____

Part of Speech	Definition or Job (how this part of speech works in a sentence)	Questions this part of speech answers, or list of examples	Tips and Clues
Noun			
Pronoun			
Adjective			
Verb			
Adverb			

Part of Speech	Definition or Job (how this part of speech works in a sentence)	Questions this part of speech answers, or list of examples	Tips and Clues
Preposition			
Conjunction			
Interjection			

Name _____

A **noun** names a _____, _____, _____, or _____.

I. Common and Proper Nouns

Common nouns name general people, places, and things:

> General people: *boy, girl, woman, man, doctor, teacher, mechanic*
> General places: *park, school, hospital, library, city, state, country*
> General things: *book, kite, building, telephone, pencil, animal, language*
> General ideas: *love, freedom, tact, sensitivity, courage, construction*

Common nouns are not _____.

Some nouns name particular or specific people or places:

> Particular people: *John Smith, Dr. Jones, Mrs. Adams*
> Particular places: *Klamm Park, KU Medical Center, Kansas City*
> Particular things: *The Brotherhood Building, City Hall, English*

These are called **proper nouns**. Proper nouns are always _____.

Practice: Underline all the nouns in the following sentences.

1. The telephone rang and rang.

2. Mr. Meier teaches our last class.

3. English is my favorite subject.

4. When the train arrives, you need to get on.

5. Her computer is always freezing up.

6. She received an award for bravery in the face of danger.

7. His anger caused him some trouble in that situation.

Which of the nouns you underlined are proper nouns? _____

_____

Which of the nouns you underlined name ideas? _____

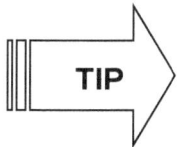

_____

> **TIP** ⟩ Sometimes, the same word can be used as different parts of speech. You have to determine how the word is being used in the sentence to know which part of speech it is in that sentence. For example, we usually think of the word "board" as a noun. We think of it as a thing, a wooden plank. However, what is the meaning of the word "board" in the following sentence?

> *You must **board** your plane now.*

In the above sentence, **board** names an action, not a thing. It is not a noun in that sentence. Let's try another sentence with the same word:

> *We put a **board** table together quickly.*

In the above sentence, **board** does not name an action or a thing. The word **board** tells what kind of table, so **board** is not a noun in that sentence either. Is **board** a noun in this next sentence?

> *He had to nail a **board** to the foundation of the deck.*

The word **board** names a thing in that sentence, so it is a noun. Remember to always determine how the word is being used in a particular sentence before you identify its part of speech.

In which of the following sentences is the word **drawing** a noun? Explain.

    a. She is **drawing** a sketch of her sister.
    b. The nurse was **drawing** blood for a lab.
    c. He asked her to sign the **drawing** she made.
    d. The group held a **drawing** to promote their cause.

In which of the following sentences is the word **dream** a noun? Explain.

     a. His **dream** was about being chased through water.
     b. Being the mayor was his **dream** job.
     c. We **dream** of a better society.
     d. She had a **dream** about drowning.

II. Singular and Plural Nouns

A noun that names one person, place, or thing is a _____ noun. A

noun that names more than one person, place or thing is a _____

noun.   Most plural nouns are formed by _____ _____ _____ .

    Examples: more than one leg = _____

                  more than one book = _____

                  more than one cat = _____

A.   Nouns that end in **–ch, –x,** or **–s** form their plurals by adding _____.

    Examples: more than one church = _____

                  more than one box = _____

                  more than one kiss = _____

B.   Some noun plurals are formed by changing the entire word.

    Examples: more than one child = _____

                  more than one man = _____

                  more than one woman = _____

                  more than one leaf = _____

Practice: Fill in the missing singular or plural form of the nouns in the following chart:

Singular	Plural
child	children
goose	
woman	
	men
	books
cave	
	knives
wife	
	ladies
cookie	
	oxen

Some singular nouns actually name groups of people or things. A group, by definition, includes more than one member, but group nouns are treated as if they are singular because they refer to one group, such as **team, council, audience, band, class.**

These are called _____ nouns. Can you think of more examples?

_____

These collective nouns can also become plural.

    <u>Examples</u>:   more than one team = teams

                  more than one class = _____

                  more than one family = _____

Nouns that end in –y usually form their plural by changing the _____ to

_____ and adding _____.

    <u>Examples</u>:   more than one lady = _____

                  more than one baby = _____

                  more than one duty = _____

Practice: Underline all the nouns you can find in the following sentences. Be careful not to call a word a noun if it is not acting like a noun in the sentence.

1. The dog and cat left muddy paw prints on the kitchen floor.

2. The editorial page was long today and focused on politics.

3. Lynette sewed the button onto her coat.

4. Did you see the 1964 Thunderbird in the parking lot?

5. After last season, we were ready for the Jayhawks to win.

6. Her book fell in the puddle and was ruined.

7. You can renew your driver's license at the Department of Motor Vehicles.

8. Math and Science are my favorite subjects at Arrowhead Middle School.

9. The sixth-graders learned to open their lockers quickly.

10. The eighth-graders take Algebra and Geometry.

11. List all the **proper nouns** you underlined in the above sentences:

_____

12. List all the **plural nouns** you underlined in the above sentences:

_____

Directions: Write a complete sentence that includes at least one common noun and one proper noun. Make sure your sentence has appropriate capitalization and punctuation. Write a *c* above your **common noun** and a *p* above your **proper noun**.

_____

_____

III. Possessive Noun Forms

Possessive noun forms show _____. For example, the

possessive form of the noun "man" is _____.

Example: *The man's coat is dirty*.

You can probably tell how to make a noun show possession: You simply add

_____ to the noun.

Practice: Let's try it. Add an *apostrophe s* to each of the following words to turn them into possessive nouns.

1. the woman_____ hat   2. the child_____ toy

3. the cat_____ bowl   4. the piano_____ keys

5. the fan_____ blades   6. the table_____ legs

IV. Plural Possessives

Remember that some nouns' plurals are made by simply _____ _____

(such as cats, dogs, tables, fans, books, arms, trees, flowers, buildings). To

make these plural nouns show possession, you simply add the apostrophe

_____ the "s" at the end of the plural noun.

Example: both *cats'* collars
all the *dogs'* leashes
many of the *books'* covers

Other nouns' plurals are made by _____ _____ _____

altogether (such as women, men, children, knives, wives, ladies, geese,

oxen). To form the possessives of these plural nouns, you add an _____ to

the plural nouns that do not end in "s" (women's, men's, children's) but you

add only the _____ to the plural nouns that end in "s" (knives',

wives', ladies').

Examples: all the oxen_____ legs

all the leaves _____ colors

all the cookies _____ containers

all the children _____ toys

Practice with Noun Plurals and Possessives

Practice: Try to edit the paragraph below to make it fit the rules of Academic English. There are 10 changes you need to make. Circle each change you need to make, then rewrite the paragraph in Academic English on the lines below.

Answer: *One of your duty is to watch the children every morning for the*

womens. Once the mens come in for lunch, you can put the childrens

down for a nap. The children toys will be stored in boxs that once held

the ladie's hat's or the mens' boot's.

_____

_____

_____

_____

_____

_____

_____

_____

_____

_____

Parts of Speech: PRONOUNS   Name _____

A **pronoun** is a word that _____ _____ _____ of a

_____. This means that a pronoun acts just like a noun in a sentence.

I. Personal Pronoun
A word that takes the place of one or more nouns.

A pronoun that takes the place of the noun "boy" would be **he** or **him**.
A pronoun that takes the place of the noun "girl" would be **she** or **her**.
A pronoun that takes the place of the noun "park" or "school" would be **it**.
A pronoun that takes the place of more than one noun might be **they** or **them** or **we** or **us**.
I and **me** are personal pronouns also. These words take the place of my own name, obviously, if I am writing about myself, or a character's name if he or she is speaking about himself or herself.

The noun that the pronoun takes the place of is called the

_____ of the pronoun. Let's state that another way: **The antecedent is the noun that the pronoun refers to.**

Practice: Circle all the personal pronouns in the following sentences. On the blank, write the **antecedent** of each pronoun. Remember that the antecedent of the pronoun is the noun to which the pronoun refers.

1. The game was challenging, but it was fun. _____

2. Although he played for years, Ted wasn't very good. _____

3. Marcus and Joe couldn't afford the movie, so they just walked

around the mall. _____

4. If Linda doesn't show up, she will be cut from the

team. _____

5. Because we were bored, Rosey and I left early. _____

6. His anger had been causing him trouble, so Rex stayed calm.

_____

II. Indefinite Pronoun

A word that refers to a general group. It has no specific antecedent.

Example: *Nobody* wants to play centerfield.
             Nobody is an indefinite pronoun.

Other indefinite pronouns are: *someone, somebody, no one, anyone, all, few, nothing, one, many, everyone, everything*.

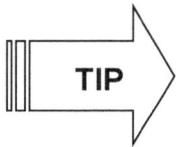

TIP Don't forget! You have to determine how the word is being used in a sentence to know which part of speech it is in that context. The words *few*, *one*, and *many* can also be used as adjectives that tell "how many" about a noun. But when these words are used in place of a noun, then they are functioning as pronouns.

Practice: Circle the indefinite pronouns in these sentences. Be careful. Some of these words act as adjectives in the following sentences.

1. Many came to the protest, but few stayed longer than an hour.

2. Many people came to the protest.

3. Somebody tried to crash the wedding.

4. We wanted to find out if anyone knew who it was.

5. All of us studied for the test.

6. All voters had to stand in line.

7. No one talked during the fire drill.

III. Possessive Pronouns

A possessive pronoun shows ownership. Some possessive pronouns are *mine, my, your, yours, their, theirs*.

When a possessive pronoun is used to modify a noun (such as "*their* house" in the example above, the possessive pronoun is functioning as an adjective).

> Example: Their house is next to **ours**.
>   That seat is **mine**.

Please note that the word "mines" is not used in Academic English. Use "mine" instead.

Practice: Circle the possessive pronouns in the following sentences.

1. The car with the dented bumper is mine.

2. Ours is the house at the end of the block.

3. He told me the book was yours, but I didn't believe him.

4. The dog roaming the neighborhood was theirs.

5. My auntie promised to take us to the show.

6. Their house is next to ours.

IV. Reflexive Pronouns

Reflexive pronouns always end in *-self* or *–selves* and refer back to a noun or pronoun in the same sentence.

> Example: Maria should buy **herself** a new notebook.
>   (**Herself** is a reflexive pronoun referring back to *Maria*.)

Other reflexive pronouns are: **myself, yourself, herself, himself, themselves ourselves.**

Practice: Circle the reflexive pronouns in the following sentences. Draw an arrow to the noun (or pronoun) to which the reflexive pronouns refers.

1. Dr. Gordon poured himself a cup of coffee.

2. The students gave themselves a pat on the back for their good grades.

3. I wanted to buy myself a treat for staying on my diet.

4. She knew James referred to himself as a great player.

5. Our whole team bought ourselves matching warm-ups.

V. Demonstrative Pronouns

A demonstrative pronoun points out one or more people or things.

Example: Whose glove is *that*?
            (*That* is a demonstrative pronoun pointing out the noun "glove".)

Other demonstrative pronouns are: **this, those, these.**

Again, when a demonstrative pronoun <u>refers to</u> or <u>modifies</u> a noun in the sentence, rather than takes the place of a noun, that pronoun is functioning as an <u>adjective</u>. The definition of a pronoun is that it <u>takes the place</u> of a noun.

Example: *That* glove belongs to her.
            (*That* is an adjective telling which glove.)

            That is her glove.
            (*That* is a pronoun, taking the place of the word "glove".)

Please note that in Academic English the pronoun "them" is not a demonstrative pronoun. Instead of using "them" (as in, "them kids", "them books", or "them papers"), use "those" (as in, "those kids", "those books", "those papers").

Practice: Circle the demonstrative pronoun in each of the following sentences.

1. She wanted those to be the only shoes her bridesmaids wore.

2. Give her this to make her skin clear.

3. These are the best steaks you can buy in this city.

4. How can you give into that?

Pronouns At-a-Glance

Personal Pronouns:	*he, she, him, her, it, they, we, us, them, you*
Indefinite Pronouns:	*nobody, someone, somebody, no one, anyone, all, few, nothing, one, many, everyone, everything*
Possessive Pronouns:	*mine, my, your, yours, their, theirs*
Reflexive Pronouns:	*myself, yourself, herself, himself, themselves ourselves*
Demonstrative Pronouns:	*this, that, these, those*

Practice: *Circle all the pronouns you can find in the following sentences. The number in parentheses tells how many pronouns are in each sentence. In your mind, try to determine which kind of pronoun each is. After the exercise, you will be asked to identify some pronouns by their category name (personal, indefinite, possessive, reflexive, or demonstrative).*

1. I started playing with that team last summer. (1)

2. Before long, you will know how to play well too. (1)

3. People trying to cross the street may not know they have to use the light. (1)

4. He was giving us a very clear signal to sit down. (2)

5. They wanted to surprise their father for Father's Day. (2)

6. We couldn't get our feet to move fast enough. (2)

7. Nobody knew what the score was after we left the park. (2)

8. They asked themselves if they could have done a better job. (3)

9. Few knew how to finish the product better than he did. (2)

10. Many were trying to ring a toy, but nobody could do it. (3)

11. Someone tripped the running boy so that he fell down and cried. (2)

12. That was the stupidest move you could make. (2)

13. They took themselves out of the running when it looked like they would lose. (4)

Of the pronouns you underlined in the sentences above, list as many as you can from each category below.

Personal Pronouns	Indefinite Pronouns	Possessive Pronouns	Reflexive Pronouns	Demonstrative Pronouns

Practice: In each blank below, write one complete sentence that contains an example of each kind of pronoun. Circle the pronoun.

(personal) 1. _____

(indefinite) 2. _____

(possessive) 3. _____

(reflexive) 4. _____

(demonstrative) 5 . _____

Parts of Speech: **ADJECTIVES**   Name _____

An adjective is a modifier, which means it describes, or gives more information about another part of speech in a sentence.

Adjectives give more information about _____ (and sometimes about pronouns).

An adjective will always answer one of three questions about a noun:

1. _____ _____?

2. _____ _____?

3. _____ _____? or _____ _____?

Example: ***a red apple***
- "apple" is a noun
- "red" is an adjective that tells <u>what kind?</u>
- <u>What kind</u> of apple? A <u>red</u> apple.

Practice: Underline the adjective in each sentence. Draw a line to the noun it describes. On the line, write which of the three questions listed above is answered by that adjective:

1. Lawyers are usually intelligent people. _____

2. We knocked down ten pins. _____

3. She slept on a soft pillow. _____

4. Twelve columns lined the entrance. _____

5. The first president was George Washington. _____

6. Everyone had a cold glass of tea. _____

Articles: The words "a", "an", and "the" are called articles. When used with a noun, they answer some of the same questions adjectives answer about the noun, so they are considered adjectives as well.

Examples: *the* tower, *a* pencil, *an* answer

> **Please note that using "a" with any word beginning with a vowel is not Academic English. Instead of "a apple", "a orange", "a envelope", or "a album", use "an apple", "an orange", "an envelope", or "an album".**

Predicate Adjectives:

A predicate adjective adds information about the subject of a sentence, but it does not appear in the sentence right next to that noun or pronoun.

Instead, a predicate adjective will appear in the sentence after a linking verb. The linking verb links the predicate adjective to the subject of the sentence.

Example: **The man was short.**
"Short" is an adjective that describes the man, and it appears after the linking verb "was".

Example: **We were cold.**
"Cold" is an adjective that describes the subject "We", and it appears after the linking verb "were".

Practice: Underline the predicate adjective in each sentence. Draw a line from the predicate adjective to the noun it modifies.

1. The dollars looked silver.

2. Her aunt sounded happy.

3. We are tired and hungry.

4. Your sister is cute.

5. The diving judge was unfair.

6. She thought the book was boring.

Proper Adjective

Sometimes a _____ _____ behaves like an adjective in a sentence. You will remember that proper nouns are capitalized. So are proper adjectives. *If a word looks like a proper noun, but it is describing a noun, then it is actually a proper adjective.*

Example: **The Louisiana gumbo was delicious.**
         "Louisiana" is capitalized because it is usually a proper noun, but in this sentence it tells *what kind* of gumbo. "What kind?" is a question that adjectives answer, so "Louisiana" is a proper adjective in this sentence.

Example: **That new car body has a Trans Am look to it.**
         What kind of look? A Trans Am look. Trans Am is the name of a particular car, a proper noun, in most instances. But in this sentence, "Trans Am" is used to tell *what kind* of look the car had, so it is a proper adjective.

Practice: In the following sentence, find the capitalized word that is acting like a proper noun or a proper adjective. Underline it. On the blank, write whether that word is acting as a proper noun or as a proper adjective.

1. The Arrowhead cafeteria serves pizza.   Proper _____

2. The best school is Smith Middle School.   Proper _____

3. We went to Denver on vacation.   Proper _____

4. Our Denver relatives are coming to visit.   Proper _____

5. His shirt shows an American eagle.   Proper _____

6. He is an American.   Proper _____

7. They are from Atlanta, Georgia.   Proper _____

8. She loves the Georgia peaches.   Proper _____

Practice: Underline each adjective. Draw an arrow from each adjective to the noun or pronoun it modifies. The number following each sentence tells how many adjectives are in that sentence. For this exercise, do <u>not</u> include the articles **a, an,** or **the**.

1. The tiny girl won first prize in the dance contest. (3)

2. The author once wrote humorous stories for children's magazines. (2)

3. A thousand pounds of birdseed were delivered to the farmer. (1)

4. The painting seemed authentic and expensive. (2)

5. Those striped tiger cubs crawled all over their patient mother. (3)

6. The professional ball player made a million dollars. (3)

7. Honeybees are busy, and they are deaf. (2)

8. Shrimp are actually quite noisy. (1)

9. Bald eagles are not really bald. (2)

10. Certain sharks are always hungry. (2)

11. The loser looked happier than the winner. (1)

12. He was the happiest contestant of all. (1)

13. Dogs are more popular pets than snakes. (1)

14. No toothpaste does a better job than Crest. (2)

15. That comedian is sillier than other comedians on t.v. (3)

16. Have you ever gone on a Carnival Cruise ship? (1)

17. Those are Washington apples. (1)

Review:

1. List three nouns from question #1 above:

_____, _____, _____

2. What is the antecedent for the pronoun "they" in question #7?

_____

3. Find one proper noun in the sentences above and write it in this blank:

_____

Using Adjectives to Improve Writing: In the following paragraph, the adjective "nice" is overused. "Nice" is not a very effective word choice. Rewrite the paragraph on the lines below. Wherever you see the word "nice", use a more descriptive adjective than "nice." Underline every adjective you choose to replace the word "nice" in the paragraph.

The candidate, dressed in a <u>nice</u> suit, stood up on the <u>nice</u> platform. "Thank you! Thank you!" the candidate shouted. "I want to thank all of you <u>nice</u> voters. Without you, I would not have been elected governor of this <u>nice</u> state. Of course, I also want to thank all the <u>nice</u> members of my staff – especially my <u>nice</u> campaign manager. I'd like to thank these <u>nice</u> members of the press, too." Then the candidate pointed to a <u>nice</u> woman in the front of the crowd. "Most of all," the candidate continued, "I want to thank my <u>nice</u> wife for all of her <u>nice</u> support."

_____

_____

_____

_____

Parts of Speech: VERBS (Part 1)   Name _____

A **verb** names an _____ or expresses a _____

_____ _____ .

I. Parts of a Sentence: Complete Subject and Complete Predicate

Every sentence consists of a complete subject and a complete predicate. All of the words in the sentence belong to either the complete subject or the complete predicate.

The complete subject consists of _____ the words that tell who or what did something in the sentence.

The complete predicate consists of _____ the words that tell what the subject did.

Sample Sentence: ***The boys and girls in our class like games and snack food***.

> The complete subject of the sample sentence above is: ***The boys and girls in our class***

> The complete predicate of the sample sentence above is: ***like games and snack food***.

Directions: For each sentence below, underline the complete subject once and the complete predicate twice.

1. Aris and Marcella will text us the address of the restaurant.

2. Two squirrels scampered across the telephone wire.

3. In the summer, we all like to go to the pool.

4. The music at the skating rink was boring.

5. Our teachers compete together on a basketball team.

II. Parts of a Sentence: Simple Subject and Simple Predicate

Inside the **complete** subject is the **simple** subject. The simple subject is the word (or words) that identifies who or what the sentence is about.

Consider our sample sentence from before:

The boys and girls in our class like games and snack food.

> **To find the simple subject of a sentence, always ask yourself, "Who or what did something?"**

If we ask ourselves "Who or what did something?" in this sentence, we would have to answer "boys and girls". So "boys and girls" is the simple subject of the sentence.

Inside the **complete** predicate is the **simple** predicate. The simple predicate is simply the **verb**, a word or phrase that names what the subject did or is doing.

> **To find the verb of a sentence, you find the simple subject first, and then ask yourself, "What is [the subject] doing?" or "What did [the subject] do?"**

Let's apply this to our sample sentence. If the subject of the sentence is "boys and girls," I ask myself, "What did they – the boys and girls – do?" My answer is that they "like games and snack food."

You have to be careful because "games and snack food" are not verbs. They are things, so they are nouns. What "the boys and girls" do is "like" something. **So the verb is "like." This word names the only action they are performing in this sentence.**

Practice: Using the same practice sentences, this time, **underline once** only the simple subject in each sentence. Then **underline twice** the verb in the sentence.

---

1. Aris and Marcella will text us the address of the restaurant.

2. Two squirrels scampered across the telephone wire.

3. In the summer, we all like to go to the pool.

4. The music at the skating rink was boring.

5. Our teachers compete together on a kickball team.

III. Categories of Verbs

Verbs can be categorized a number of ways. Some of these categories are:
- Action Verbs vs. Linking Verbs
- Main Verbs vs. Helping Verbs
- Regular Verbs vs. Irregular Verbs

It is not terribly critical for you to be able to identify which category a verb represents, but **working with the categories will help you to become familiar with the kinds of ways verbs are used in a sentence**. You will become more adept at identifying the verb of the sentence, which is critical for sentence analysis and for improving your own writing.

IV. Action Verbs vs. Linking Verbs

Remember that the definition of a verb is a word (or words) that expresses

the _____ that the subject performs or that indicates the subject's

_____ _____ _____.

A verb that names an action is called an _____ _____.

      Ex. Action Verbs: *John **works** at the main office.*
                                      *The pen **dripped** ink on her shirt.*

Sometimes the action is one you cannot see:

      Ex. Action Verbs: *Gianni **has** a problem.*
                                        *My mom **thought** about the question.*

A verb that names a state of being is called a _____ _____.

Linking verbs do not tell of an action. They express a state of being. They are called linking verbs because they _____ the subject with some other word in the sentence.

The most common linking verbs are these:

> **be (am, is, are, was, were, been, being)**
> **become   seem   feel   taste**
> **look   sound   grow**
> **appear   smell**

Ex. Linking Verbs: *John **is** a builder.*
                                   *The air **seems** smoky.*

Many linking verbs can also be used as action verbs.

Ex.   Linking Verb: *Marcia **felt** tired.*
           Action Verb: *Marcia **felt** the cat's fur.*

Ex.   Linking Verb: *The cake **tasted** wonderful.*
           Action Verb: *The cook **tasted** his sauce.*

Whether the verb is action or linking depends on whether or not the subject is performing the action of the verb. If the subject ("Marcia" or "The cook") "felt" or "tasted" something, then those verbs are action verbs.

Practice: In each sentence below, underline the subject once and the verb twice. In the space, write *Action* or *Linking* to tell what kind of verb it is.

> Review: What question do you ask yourself to find the subject of a sentence?

_____ 1. Water dropped from the sky.

_____ 2. The water felt cool and refreshing.

_____ 3. The students waited for their teacher on the sidewalk.

_____ 4. His bike is shiny and new.

_____ 5. The baby made a cooing sound.

_____ 6. I washed the dishes after breakfast.

_____ 7. He always looks happy.

_____ 8. We looked at the sky for a long time.

_____ 9. He ate all the chips in the giant bag.

_____ 10. They grew corn in their backyard.

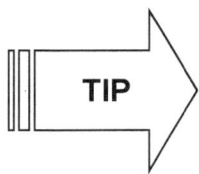

TIP ⟩ When you can't figure out if a word is being used as a linking verb or an action verb, just substitute the word "***seem***" for the verb in question. If the sentence makes sense, the verb is a ***linking verb***. If the sentence does not make sense when you substitute "seem" for the verb, then the verb is an ***action verb***.

<u>Here's how it works</u>: The verb in the sample sentence below is "look." I don't know if "look" is being used as a linking verb or an action verb in this sentence. Watch what happens when I replace the word "seem" for the verb "look."

Example 1:   ***I look tired.***   ***I seem tired.***

(The sentence makes sense after I substitute "seem". "Look" must be a **linking verb** in example 1.)

Example 2:   ***We look at books.***   ***We seem at books.***
(The sentence does not make sense when I substitute "seem". "Look" must be an **action verb** in example 2.)

V. Main Verb vs. Helping Verb

A verb often consists of more than one word. A main verb in a sentence may

have one or more _____ verbs with it. All the words in the verb (the

main verb plus the helping verbs) make up the _____ _____.

Here are the helping verbs, shown with the action verb "go":

will go	*can* go	*would* go	*could* go	*must* go
shall go	*may* go	*did* go	*is* going	*do* go
have gone	*has* gone	*might* go		

Please note that the verb forms "had went" or "have went" are not used in Academic English. Use "went" without a helping verb, as in "He *went* to the store." Use "gone" with "had" or "has", as in "He *had gone* to the store" or "He *has gone* to the store."

The words that make up a verb phrase are sometimes interrupted by other words that are not verbs:

should not *have called*   *will* probably *call*
may never *call*   *could* hardly *see*
might really *like*   *would* likely *believe*

BONUS: Can you tell what part of speech these words are that interrupt the

verb? _____

Practice: Identify the parts of the verb phrase in each sentence by writing **mv** over the main verb and **hv** over every helping verb.

   1. He will follow the ambulance.

2. Cecil could hardly finish his sandwich.

3. We could not have predicted the outcome of the movie.

4. Will you come to my house this afternoon?

5. Can I make an appointment with the doctor?

6. We might have been singing on stage by then.

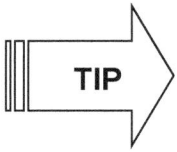

TIP Turn a question into a statement to analyze the parts. For example, turn the question, "Will you come to my house this afternoon?" into the statement, "You will come to my house this afternoon." It is easier to find the correct subject and verb in a statement.

Practice: The following sentences have main verbs but no helping verbs. Choose a helping verb that makes sense and write it in the blank for each sentence.

1. You _____ never get that problem right.

2. _____ you throw a long pass?

3. They _____ _____ read the chapter by then.

4. I _____ taking the trash out right now.

5. They _____ bring in the trash barrels later tonight.

6. We _____ have _____ watching t.v. instead of waiting for you.

Parts of Speech: VERBS (Part 2)   Name _____

A **verb** names an _____ or a _____ _____ _____ .

Review VERBS (Part 1)

1. We learned that a verb that shows action is called an _____ verb, while a verb that shows state of being is called a _____ verb.

2. We learned that a verb _____ consists of the main verb and any helping verbs.

3. Words that add information to verb phrases are usually _____ (the part of speech that modifies verbs).

4. One hint for deciding whether a verb is linking or action is to substitute the word _____ for the verb. If the sentence makes sense, then the verb is a(n) _____ verb.

Practice: In each sentence, underline the subject once and the verb or verb phrase twice. After each sentence, write **A** if the verb is an action verb, or **L** if the verb is a linking verb.

1. It rains in California, but not often.   _____

2. Rain may fall daily in Oregon.   _____

3. I saw the Space Needle in Seattle.   _____

4. I felt nervous so high off the ground.   _____

5. I felt the soft texture of her coat.   _____

6. Has anyone seen my phone?   _____

7. The man in the red jacket is our coach.   _____

8. You can overcome your fears.   _____

I. The Principal Parts of a Verb

The principal parts of a verb are the four forms of the verb from which all other verb tenses are made.

In the English language, the four principal parts are:

The present (also called the base or infinitive): (to) **walk/walks**

The present participle (formed by adding – ing): **walking**

The past (formed by adding –ed): **walked**

The past participle (also formed by adding –ed, but used with "have/has/had"): (have) **walked**

Practice: Try to apply these principal parts for the verbs listed. Fill in the empty spaces by following the pattern of the sample given.

Present	Present Participle	Past	Past Participle
dance(s)	(is) dancing	danced	(have) danced
cook(s)		cooked	(have) cooked
study(ies)	(is) studying		(have) studied
count(s)	(is) counting	counted	
	(is) snowing	snowed	(has) snowed
work(s)	(is) working		
		carried	(has) carried

II. Regular Verbs vs. Irregular Verbs

Verbs that form their "past" and "past participle" by adding **–ed** are called

_____ verbs. All of the verbs in the table above are regular verbs.

Verbs that form their principal parts in other ways are called

_____verbs.

Practice: Try to finish the table by filling in the principal parts for these irregular verbs.

Present	Present Participle	Past	Past Participle
burst	(is) bursting	burst	(have) burst
cost		cost	
bring			(have) brought
	(is) catching		(have) caught
bite	(is) biting	bit	
break	(is) breaking		(have) broken
begin		began	
drink		drank	(have) drunk
sing		sang	
choose			(have) chosen

III. Verb Tenses

Tense refers to *time*. Writers show actions that occurred in the past through *past tense verbs*, actions that are occurring in the present through *present tense verbs*, and actions that will occur in the future through *future tense verbs*.

Example: The verb is "to plant."

The present tense of "to plant" is "plant" or "plants": ***I plant the seeds. He plants the seeds.***

Present tense sounds like the action occurs always and now.

The present participle of "to plant" is "planting" and is used with a helping verb "am/is/are"): ***I am planting the seeds. You are planting the seeds. He is planting the seeds.***

The past tense of "to plant" is "planted": ***Yesterday, I planted the seeds***.

You can see that this verb tense is formed by adding *–ed* to the verb "plant" to show that it happened in the past. This means that "plant" is a regular verb, of course.

The future tense of "to plant" is "will plant": ***Tomorrow, I will plant more seeds***.

You can see that this verb tense is formed by adding a helping verb "*will*" or "*shall*" to the verb "plant" to show that it will happen the near or far future.

Practice: Underline the subject in each sentence once. Underline the verb or verb phrase twice. On the line, write *present*, *past*, or *future* to tell which verb tense is being used in the sentence.

1. She finishes her homework before school. _____

2. The secretary will enroll the new students on Monday. _____

3. Everyone passed to the next grade level. _____

4. The team runs drills on the field. _____

5. We gave her our money for the trip already. _____

6. The woman will pay her electric bill next week. _____

IV. Subject-Verb Agreement

In Academic English, sentences with singular subjects have to have

_____ verbs, and sentences with plural subjects have to

have _____ verbs. This gets a little confusing since subjects that

end in "s" are often plural (*cats, dogs, toys, books*), but verbs that end in "s"

are usually present tense verbs that are singular (*cooks, drinks, breaks,*

reads).

One person (singular subject) ***drinks*** or ***eats*** or ***reads*** (singular verb).

Two people (plural subject) ***drink*** or ***eat*** or ***read*** (plural verb).

Practice: Circle the verb that agrees with the subject in number (meaning, plural or singular) in Academic English.

1. He (rake *or* rakes) the yard every Saturday.

2. The girls (cook *or* cooks) dinner for their grandparents weekly.

3. They (swim *or* swims) in the lake when they go camping.

4. The boys (mow *or* mows) grass on weekends.

5. She (do *or* does) her homework on Sunday.

Name _____

An adverb is a modifier, which means it describes, or gives more information about another part of speech in a sentence.

An adverb gives more information about a _____, an

_____, or another _____ .

An adverb will always answer one of four questions about a verb, an adjective, or another adverb:

      1. _____ ?

      2. _____ ?

      3. _____ ?

      4. _____ _____ _____?

Example: ***Yesterday, the boy rode his scooter home very quickly.***
- "Yesterday" is an adverb that tells **when** he rode his scooter.
- "home" is an adverb that tells **where** he rode his scooter.
- "quickly" is an adverb that tells **how** he rode his scooter.
- "very" is an adverb that tells **to what extent** he rode quickly.

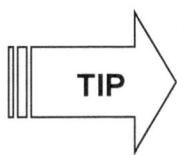

TIP ⟩ Because many adverbs tell **how** something is done, many words that end in **–ly** are adverbs, words like **quickly, harshly, slowly, sadly**, etc. But there are many adverbs that do not end in **–ly**, such as **later, today, outside, never**, etc.

The following words are always adverbs, answering "to what extent?":

              very, not, too, really

Practice: Underline the adverb in each sentence. Draw a line to the word it describes. Try to determine whether that word is a verb, an adjective, or another adverb. (If you determine that the word is a noun, then you have found an adjective, not an adverb.) On the line, write which question the adverb answers. Your choices are **When?**, **Where?**, **How?**, or **To what extent?**

1. Lawyers are usually intelligent people. _____

2. We knocked down ten pins. _____

3. She slept peacefully on a soft pillow. _____

4. Twelve columns majestically lined the entrance. _____

5. The first president was not Thomas Jefferson. _____

6. Some fish can swim backward. _____

7. Yo-yos were first used as weapons. _____

8. Junior beat the desk impatiently. _____

9. Both children came forward to claim the prize. _____

10. That car may once have belonged to us. _____

11. Later, he gave us the tape recording. _____

12. She visited her hometown occasionally. _____

13. They really wanted to see the tower. _____

14. They were able, finally, to find a seat. _____

15. He never played the game. _____

Review: Write as many pronouns as you can from the sentences above.

_____

The Comparative Form of Adverbs

The comparative form of an adverb compares two people or things.

Examples: Jack left *earlier* than we did.
  ("*earlier*" answers "*When?*")

  Mary sings *more sweetly* than Michelle does.
  ("*more sweetly*" answers "*How?*")

  Mom calls *more often* than Dad does.
  ("*more often*" answers "*When?*")

The Superlative Form of Adverbs

The superlative form of an adverb compares more than two people or things.

Examples: Of all the players, James jumps *highest*.
  ("*highest*" answers "*How?*")

  My five kids all like math, but Beth likes math *most*.
  ("*most*" answers "*To what extent?*")

  He answered *fastest* of the three contestants.
  ("*fastest*" answers "*How?*")

Remember: You can only identify a word as a certain part of speech according to how the word is being used in the sentence. Most words can be used as more than one part of speech.

Think and Respond: Would any of the words that act as adverbs in the examples above ever act as adjectives? Try to write a sentence in which each of these words acts as an adjective.

highest   1. _____

most   2. _____

fastest   3. _____

Application for your writing and editing:

In Academic English, we do not use the superlative form of adverbs or adjectives (**best, most, brightest, skinniest**) when we are comparing only two people or things.

We use the comparative form (**better, more, brighter, skinnier**) when comparing only two people or things.

We use the superlative form (**best, most, brightest, skinniest**) when comparing three or more people or things.

So which of the following usages are examples of Academic English?

1. Of the two of us, you are the smartest.

2. Of the two of us, you are the smarter.

3. Of all the people in the class, Monique is the better writer.

4. Of all the people in the class, Monique is the best writer.

Using Negatives as Adverbs

Negatives are words that give a sense of "no" or "not" in a sentence. Common negative words are **no, not, none, never, nothing, hardly, barely, scarcely**. Usually, negatives are adverbs, answering the adverb question "To what extent?"

Example 1: She will **not** go with us.

In this example, the word "**not**" answers the question "**To what extent** will she go with us?" The answer is, "**To no extent at all**" since she will **not** go.

Example 2: She can hardly stand it!

In this example, the word "**hardly**" is an adverb that answers the question "**To what extent** can she stand it?" The answer is, "**Hardly**".

Please note: In Academic English, we do not use double negatives. For example, "We ain't going to no concert" is not Academic English because it contains two negatives in the same expression: "ain't" and "no". The Academic English version of this sentence is: "We are not going to any concert."

Here is another example.

Non-Academic English: *That guy don't know nothing.*

Academic English: *That guy doesn't know anything.*
or,   *That guy knows nothing.*

Contractions ending in **–n't** (*don't, didn't, can't, won't*) are negatives. They combine a verb with "**not**" (*do not, did not, cannot, will not*). An apostrophe takes the place of the missing letter. In Academic English, we do not link a negative contraction with another negative in a sentence.

Non-Academic English: *Don't none of us know the answer.*

Academic English: *None of us know the answer.*

Practice: All of the following sentences have double negatives. Rewrite the sentences in Academic English.

1. Don't none of us like that book.

_____

2. Ain't none of us going to the game.

_____

3. We hardly had no time to get ready.

_____

4. They won't take no disrespect from nobody.

_____

5. We ain't got nothing to tell you.

_____

Practice with Adverbs

Practice: *Underline the adverbs in each of the following sentences. The number following each sentence tells how many adverbs are in that sentence. Make sure the word you underline answers one of the four questions that adverbs answer.*

1. Most players work extremely hard at their sport. (2)

2. That painting is simply magnificent. (1)

3. Her extremely expensive coat was made of fur. (1)

4. Her story is totally unbelievable. (1)

5. People rather bravely swallowed the unfamiliar food. (2)

6. Almost accidentally, she invented a radically new style of music.(3)

7. He will never accept her reason for the breakup. (1)

8. He rather sadly sang his original song. (2)

9. Scrabble has remained a very popular game for decades. (1)

10. You should never ride with a dangerous driver. (1)

11. Elvis Presley was an incredibly popular singer. (1)

12. He was driving especially dangerously on the highway. (2)

Practice: Circle the correct adverb or adjective choice in the parentheses for each sentence.

1. Of the two students, Nancy had the (***better*** or ***best***) grades.

2. Of all the kids in class, he is the (***louder*** or ***loudest***) one.

3. That group is the (***more*** or ***most***) talented of all.

4. Between you and me, I have (***curlier*** or ***curliest***) hair.

5. The (***taller*** or ***tallest***) one of the pair is Daniel.

6. He is the (***richer*** or ***richest***) of the two brothers.

Parts of Speech: PREPOSITIONS   Name _____

A **preposition** is a word that shows the _____ of one noun or pronoun to another noun or pronoun in the sentence.

     Example: *Dave climbed over the fence.*

The preposition _____ shows the relationship between

_____ and the _____. Fill in different prepositions to show

different relationships between Dave and the fence:

     Dave climbed _____ the fence.

     Dave climbed _____ the fence.

One way to understand how this part of speech functions is to name every relation or position that a book can have to a desk:

     The book can be . . .
          on the desk,
        or **in** the desk,
        or **under** the desk,
        or **above** the desk,
        or **beside** the desk,
        or **behind** the desk,
        or **beneath** the desk.

All of these words that show where the book is in relation to the chair (**on, in, under, above, beside, behind, beneath**) are prepositions.

Think of words that describe where a cat might be in relation to a tree:

The cat could be _____ the tree, or _____ the tree, or

_____ the tree, or _____ the tree, or _____ the

tree. The words you used to fill in the blanks are most likely prepositions.

Most Commonly Used Prepositions:

about	below	excepting	off	toward
above	beneath	for	on	under
across	beside(s)	from	onto	underneath
after	between	in	out	until
against	beyond	in front of	outside	up
along	but (except)	inside	over	upon
among	by	in spite of	past	up to
around	concerning	instead of	regarding	with
at	despite	into	since	within
because of	down	like	through	without
before	during	near	throughout	with regard to
behind	except	of	to	with respect to

The Prepositional Phrase

In a sentence, a preposition introduces a _____

_____.

A prepositional phrase consists of the _____, the

_____ _____ _____ _____ (which is always

a noun or pronoun), and any words between those two words.

The object of the preposition is the _____ or _____ that

ends the prepositional phrases.

> Consider this example: *The book is on the desk.*
> - The preposition *on* tells the relationship between the book and the desk.
> - *Desk* is the object of the preposition.
> - The complete prepositional phrase is *on the desk.*

When we analyze sentences, we want to be able to tell how many clauses there are and whether each clause is an independent clause or a dependent clause. To do that, we have to be able to see subject-verb combinations.

You need to know that the subject or verb of a sentence will <u>never</u> be found in a prepositional phrase.

When will the subject of a sentence be found in a prepositional phrase?

_____

When will the verb of a sentence be found in a prepositional phrase?

_____

Our marking system asks you to enclose prepositional phrases – the entire phrase – in parentheses, like this:

The book is (on the desk).

If you don't know when the phrase should end, say the preposition and then ask yourself "what?" or "whom?" In our sample sentence, you might find the preposition "on" and then ask yourself, "on what?" The answer is "the desk," so the phrase ends after "desk": *on the desk*.

The <u>object of the preposition</u> is the noun or pronoun that ends the prepositional phrase. Many prepositional phrases are only a few words in length, but prepositional phrases can be much longer. Consider this example, which includes several modifiers between the preposition ("*over*") and its object ("*fence*"):

<u>Example</u>: Dave climbed (*over the gray, sagging, splinter-filled wooden fence*).

What is the Function of a Prepositional Phrase?

In a sentence, a prepositional phrase acts as a _____ part of speech.

It can act as an _____ that tells "which one, what kind, or how many" about a noun, or it can act as an _____ that tells "when, where, how, to what extent" about a verb or another adverb.

If the prepositional phrase is acting as an adjective, it will answer one of the questions that adjectives answer. Which question does the prepositional phrase in each example answer – *how many, which one,* or *what kind*?

_____ The book (with the red cover) is mine.

_____ The book (about cars) is mine.

If the prepositional phrase is acting as an adverb, it will answer one of the questions that adverbs answer. Which question does the prepositional phrase in each example answer – *when, where, how,* or *to what extend*?

_____ The book is (on the shelf).

_____ We arrived (after ten o'clock).

_____ We arrived (in a limo).

Practice with Prepositions and Prepositional Phrases

Practice: In each of the following sentences, enclose all prepositional phrases in parentheses. The number following each sentence tells you how many prepositional phrases are in that sentence.

1. Your shoes are under the couch. (1)

2. His paper fell behind the refrigerator. (1)

3. She gave me money for gas. (1)

4. He lost his speed near the finish line. (1)

5. I took a bite of the hot and spicy chip dip. (1)

6. We will drive to the party together. (1)

7. The clothes on this rack are reduced. (1)

8. You may bring a lunch to school for the field trip. (2)

9. The photos hung on the wall above the television. (2)

10. Carla found her book inside her cluttered locker under a stack of papers.(3)

11. In the first act of the play, the actor fainted on stage! (3)

12. Outside the door of the barn, within three feet of my reach, sat a tiny kitten with white paws. (5)

13. Because of the freezing rain, our game against Coronado was cancelled. (2)

More Directions: Now go back through your sentences and mark an "o" above each object of the preposition. Remember that the object of a preposition is the noun or pronoun that ends the prepositional phrase.

Preposition or Not?

Many of the same words that are listed as prepositions on the top of page 50 are sometimes used as different parts of speech. For example, ***like*** is listed as a commonly used preposition, but we know that ***like*** can also be used as an action verb. ***The part of speech is always determined by how a word is being used in a sentence.***

Practice: In each of these sentences, decide whether the bold word is acting as a preposition or not. Write a ***p*** for ***preposition*** after the sentence if the bold word is a preposition. Write nothing if the bold word is some other part of speech. ***Hint***: If there's no prepositional phrase with it, the word is not a preposition.

1. We all **like** skating and bowling. _____

2. He enjoys active field trips, **like** skating or bowling. _____

3. She took us **to** the store. _____

4. She likes **to** go shopping alone. _____

5. The rain came **down**. _____

6. We rolled **down** the steep grassy hill. _____

7. **Inside**, the air was cool. _____

8. The air **inside** the building was cool. _____

9. Everyone tried the rope swing **but** Shauna. _____

10. We tried the rope swing, **but** we liked the tire swing better. _____

11. I asked George and Eli **over** to the house for dinner. _____

12. A cow cannot jump **over** the moon. _____

Challenge: If it's not a preposition, can you tell what part of speech the bold word is? Write it in the empty blank if you think you know. Your choices are: *adjective, adverb, verb, conjunction*. There's one *sign of an infinitive* as well.

When the Object of a Preposition is a Pronoun

Pronouns, as well as nouns, may be used as objects of prepositions. Only the objective case of pronouns can be used as objects. The objective case forms to remember are ***me, you, her, him, it, us, them***, and ***whom***.

> Example: Ann talked to ***us***. (not ***we***)
> Example: We thought of ***him***. (not ***he***)
> Example: Come with ***me***. (not ***I***)

Sometimes the object of a preposition is compound, meaning two nouns/pronouns joined by a conjunction such as ***and***.

> Example: Ann talked (to John and him).

At times, compound objects are confusing. To test compound objects, try the pronoun by itself as the object.

> Example: *Ann talked to John and **I***. vs. *Ann talked to John and **me***.

> Try each pronoun by itself:
> *Ann talked to **I***. vs. *Ann talked to **me***.

The grammatically correct sentence is:
Ann talked to John and _____.

Practice with Pronoun Objects

Practice: *Circle the correct pronoun from the two given in parentheses. Enclose each prepositional phrase in parentheses.*

1. The magician stared directly at Paul and (*I, me*).

2. Behind (*we, us*) sat a group of gigglers.

3. I received an invitation from DeeDee and (*she, her*).

4. The friendly dog lay beside (*they, them*).

5. To (*who, whom*) was that letter written?

6. There's nobody here but (*I, me*).

7. The graduates walked past (*they, them*) and (*I, me*).

8. Lights from a car came toward (*he, him*) and (*I, me*).

Becoming More Familiar with Prepositions

Directions: Below is the list of commonly used prepositions with only their beginning letters filled in. Fill in as many blanks as you can from memory, or from your knowledge of how prepositions function. Before you look back in your packet to find the prepositions, try to figure them out by asking yourself which words beginning with the given letter might complete the following examples:

We walked _____ the street.

We left _____ the show was over.

The horse stood _____ the trees.

a_____	b_____	e_____	o_____	t_____
a_____	b_____	f_____	o_____	u_____
a_____	b_____	f_____	o_____	u_____
a_____	b_____	i_____	o_____	u_____
a_____	b_____	i_____	o_____	u_____
a_____	b_____	i_____	o_____	u_____
a_____	b_____	i_____	p_____	u_____
a_____	c_____	i_____	r_____	w_____
a_____	d_____	i_____	s_____	w_____
b_____	d_____	l_____	t_____	w_____
b_____	d_____	n_____	t_____	w_____
b_____	e_____	o_____	t_____	w_____

Recap on Prepositions:

- When we analyze or mark parts of sentences, we first enclose prepositional phrases in parentheses since every phrase acts as a single part of speech.

- The entire prepositional phrase acts as an adjective or an adverb.

- The subject of the sentence is never in a prepositional phrase.

- The verb of the sentence is never in a prepositional phrase.

- The prepositional phrase consists of the preposition, the object of the preposition, and all the words in between the preposition and its object.

- When the object of a preposition is a pronoun (instead of a noun), it must be written in the objective case.

Below are three more sets of blanks for you to practice memorizing commonly used prepositions, if you like. You could race your classmates to see who can think of the most prepositions in five minutes. You could compare your list with a partner to see which ones you tend to remember and which ones he or she tends to remember. Or, just practice by yourself.

a_____	b_____	e_____	o_____	t_____
a_____	b_____	f_____	o_____	u_____
a_____	b_____	f_____	o_____	u_____
a_____	b_____	i_____	o_____	u_____
a_____	b_____	i_____	o_____	u_____
a_____	b_____	i_____	o_____	u_____
a_____	b_____	i_____	p_____	u_____
a_____	c_____	i_____	r_____	w_____
a_____	d_____	i_____	s_____	w_____
b_____	d_____	l_____	t_____	w_____
b_____	d_____	n_____	t_____	w_____
b_____	e_____	o_____	t_____	w_____

a_____	b_____	e_____	o_____	t_____
a_____	b_____	f_____	o_____	u_____
a_____	b_____	f_____	o_____	u_____
a_____	b_____	i_____	o_____	u_____
a_____	b_____	i_____	o_____	u_____
a_____	b_____	i_____	o_____	u_____
a_____	b_____	i_____	p_____	u_____
a_____	c_____	i_____	r_____	w_____
a_____	d_____	i_____	s_____	w_____
b_____	d_____	l_____	t_____	w_____
b_____	d_____	n_____	t_____	w_____
b_____	e_____	o_____	t_____	w_____

a_____	b_____	e_____	o_____	t_____
a_____	b_____	f_____	o_____	u_____
a_____	b_____	f_____	o_____	u_____
a_____	b_____	i_____	o_____	u_____
a_____	b_____	i_____	o_____	u_____
a_____	b_____	i_____	o_____	u_____
a_____	b_____	i_____	p_____	u_____
a_____	c_____	i_____	r_____	w_____
a_____	d_____	i_____	s_____	w_____
b_____	d_____	l_____	t_____	w_____
b_____	d_____	n_____	t_____	w_____
b_____	e_____	o_____	t_____	w_____

Preposition or Adverb

Several words that are used as prepositions are also used as adverbs. If the word begins a phrase, it is probably a preposition. You will not have a preposition without a prepositional phrase. If the word is used without a phrase, it is probably an adverb.

Example #1: We walked **outside**.
"Outside" is an adverb, telling *where* we walked.

Example #2: We colored **outside** the lines.
"Outside" is a preposition, beginning the phrase "outside the lines".

Example #3: The balloon went **up**.
"Up" is an adverb.

Example #4: The balloon went **up** the chimney.
"Up the chimney" is a prepositional phrase.

Practice: On the blank line after each sentence, write whether the word in italics is being used as an adverb or a preposition. If you write that the word is a preposition, then enclose the prepositional phrase in parentheses.

1. Come *into* the school right now. _____

2. She fell *down* at the finish line. _____

3. When the bus stopped, three kids got *off*. _____

4. Maybe we should wait *inside* since it is raining. _____

5. I have heard that song *before*. _____

6. Can you see *out* the window? _____

7. The Brown family arrived just *before* twelve. _____

8. At 5:30 a.m., her alarm went *off*. _____

9. Her books fell *off* the desk. _____

10. The kitten rolled *over*. _____

11. The truck rolled *over* the newspaper. _____

12. *Near* the school is a public library. _____

Parts of Speech: CONJUNCTIONS   *Name* _____

A conjunction is a word that connects words or groups of words. The most

commonly used conjunctions are _____, _____, and _____ .

There are several kinds of conjunctions – coordinating conjunctions, subordinating conjunctions, correlative conjunctions, and conjunctive adverbs. We will learn and practice each kind separately.

Coordinating Conjunctions: _____, _____, _____,

_____, _____, _____, _____. Some people use the mnemonic (memory) device "FANBOYS" to remember the first letter of each of the seven coordinating conjunctions.

Directions: Circle the coordinating conjunctions in the following sentences.

1. The fans cheered and clapped for the home team.

2. Daffy Duck and Tweety Bird are Disney characters.

3. You may use a pencil or a pen to sign the document.

4. Our vacation was short but sweet.

5. He was cold so he put on a jacket.

6. He arrived late, for he had missed his ride.

7. She was injured, yet she played the whole game.

8. We cannot attend, nor can our parents.

9. He got a consequence, for he had forgotten his homework.

10. He had forgotten his homework, so he got a consequence.

   • The use of the word "for" as a conjunction is rare. The word "for" is most often used as a preposition. In sentence number 1, is the word "for" a conjunction or a preposition? How do you know?

Correlative Conjunctions:

Correlative conjunctions are pairs of words used to join sentence parts. The two parts of the correlative conjunction do not appear in the sentence altogether. They have other words between them. That's why, when we list them, we use an ellipsis (three dots: . . .) to indicate that there would be other words between the parts of the correlative conjunctions.

The correlative conjunctions are: _____ . . . _____ ,

_____ . . . _____ , _____ . . . _____ ,

_____ . . . _____ , _____ . . . _____ .

Practice: Find these pairs of conjunctions in the sentences below. Circle the words that make up the correlative conjunctions.

1. He led the team not only in free throws but also in rebounds.

2. Both the girls and the boys played soccer.

3. She is not a cheerleader but a dancer.

4. Either we go to the show, or we give back the tickets.

5. Neither the internet nor the phone was working during the storm.

6. We could not decide whether to go or stay home.

7. She won not only a scholarship but also ten thousand dollars.

8. We wanted either steak or chicken.

9. She could see neither the stoplight nor the police siren.

10. Whether he wins or not, he played a fantastic game.

11. It was not a leaf but a baby bird that fell from the tree.

12. The thieves took both the t.v. and the computer.

Subordinating Conjunctions:

A subordinating conjunction comes at the beginning of a subordinate (or dependent clause) and establishes the relationship between the dependent clause and the rest of the sentence. The subordinating conjunction also turns that clause into something that depends on the rest of the sentence for its meaning.

Common Subordinating Conjunctions

after	if	though
although	if only	til
as	in order that	unless
as if	now that	until
as long as	once	when
as though	whenever	
because	since	where
before	so that	whereas
even if	than	wherever
even though	that	while

If it does not introduce, or start, a subordinate clause, the word is not a subordinating conjunction. So what is a clause? **A clause is a group of words that contains a subject and a verb.** So a subordinate clause starts with a subordinating conjunction and contains a subject and its verb. Because the clause is subordinate, it has to be attached to a main clause, or an independent clause, which is a sentence that can stand by itself.

Here's how this all works:

After he bathed the dog, he dried it carefully with a towel.

- "After" is the subordinating conjunction that introduces the subordinate clause "After he bathed the dog." *Circle "after."*
- Since "after he bathed the dog" cannot stand alone as a sentence, it is attached to the main clause "he dried it carefully with a towel." *Enclose the subordinate clause "After he bathed the dog," in brackets.*
- In the subordinate clause, "he" is the subject (*underline once*) and "bathed" is the verb (*underline twice*). In the main clause, "he" is the subject (*underline once*), and "dried" is the verb (*underline twice*).

- Since the subordinate clause comes before the main clause, it is followed by a comma. If the main clause came first, and then the subordinate clause, you would not use a comma.
- One main clause + one or more subordinate clauses = a complex sentence.

Practice: Here are several sentences with subordinating conjunctions. Circle the subordinating conjunctions, and put brackets around the entire subordinate clause (the clause that goes with the subordinating conjunction).

Ex. *He dried the dog carefully with a towel [(after) he bathed it].*
Ex. *[(After) he bathed the dog], he dried it carefully with a towel.*

1. Because we held the record, everyone wanted to beat us.

2. I gave him a VIP pass so that he could go to the Renaissance Rally.

3. We take the flag inside before we go home.

4. As long as you sign up, you can go on the field trip.

5. Whatever you are planning, you must tell the supervisor.

6. Until you can give a good excuse, your absence will be unexcused.

7. We did not know when he would return.

8. Though we practiced, our song was not good.

9. We always wondered if you wrote that rap.

10. Now that we have finished the dishes, you can put them away.

11. We heard that Janelle broke her ankle.

12. He got a higher score than you would believe.

13. Once he could take a few deep breaths, we knew that he would be okay.

14. I will have to guess the answer since you won't tell me.

15. When you get home, I want you to dust and vacuum.

- Notice how a comma is used right after the subordinate clause when the subordinate clause starts the sentence. Write the number of all those sentences in this blank:

_____

- When a sentence contains one main clause plus one subordinate clause, it is called <u>a complex sentence</u>.

Conjunctive Adverbs: Conjunctions connect words, phrases or clauses. When the job of an adverb is to connect ideas, we call them conjunctive adverbs.

Common Conjunctive Adverbs

accordingly	however	nevertheless
also	indeed	otherwise
besides	instead	similarly
consequently	likewise	still
conversely	meanwhile	subsequently
finally	moreover	then
furthermore	nevertheless	therefore
hence	next	thus

A conjunctive adverb can join two main clauses. When you use a conjunctive adverb to join main clauses, you have to <u>use a semi-colon before the conjunctive adverb and a comma after the conjunctive adverb</u>.

Ex. The dark skies discouraged Zach from running; moreover, he had a lot of homework to finish.

- Notice that the conjunctive adverb – *moreover* - comes right between the two independent clauses. It is literally joining two complete sentences together.
- Notice how the conjunctive adverb – *moreover* – is punctuated with a semi-colon before it and a comma after it.

- Notice that the two clauses are indeed independent, or main, clauses. Each can stand alone as a complete sentence because each has a subject and its verb:

S	V		S	V
skies	discouraged		he	had

Practice: In the next three examples, circle the conjunctive adverb. Underline the subject in each clause once and the verb in each clause twice.

1. Lane's apartment is small; otherwise, he would have bought a dog.

2. The teacher gave us lots of practice problems; consequently, we were ready for the test.

3. She lied about the incident; besides, she wasn't even there at the time.

4. John hated to miss the game; however, he had to work late that night.

5. We didn't like babysitting her niece; nevertheless, we volunteered to do it.

A writer might also use a conjunctive adverb to <u>introduce, interrupt, or conclude</u> a single main clause. In these cases, you will often need commas to separate the conjunctive adverb from the rest of the sentence.

Here are some examples of conjunctive adverbs used with single main clauses:

1) At 10 a.m., Paul was supposed to be taking his biology midterm. **Instead,** he was sound asleep at home.

2) Maria refused Jeff's third invitation to go out. This young man is determined, **nevertheless,** to take her to dinner one night soon.

3) After mowing the yard in the hot sun, Jose was too tired to shower. He did wash his hands, **however**.

Practice: For each sentence below, circle the conjunctive adverb. Fill in the correct punctuation for the use of the conjunctive adverb.

1. Erin plays a solo in every concert still she becomes nervous before each performance.

2. We planned to eat at McDonald's instead we ended up at Taco Bell.

3. He wrote one of the best essays in the class therefore he was nominated for newspaper editor.

4. We waited for hours finally they came walking around the corner.

5. Janine baked chocolate cupcakes for the club. Similarly Maryann brought brownies.

6. We tried hard to follow the directions to the theater. We turned right on 18ᵗʰ Street accordingly.

- *For extra practice with the same sentences, try to do the following:*
  - *Enclose all prepositional phrases in parentheses*
  - *Underline the subjects once and the verbs twice*
  - *List two adjectives: _____ _____*
  - *List three pronouns: _____ _____ _____*

1. Erin plays a solo in every concert still she becomes nervous before each performance.

2. We planned to eat at McDonald's instead we ended up at Taco Bell.

3. He wrote one of the best essays in the class therefore he was nominated for newspaper editor.

4. We waited for hours finally they came walking around the corner.

5. Janine baked chocolate cupcakes for the club. Similarly Maryann brought brownies.

6. We tried hard to follow the directions to the theater. We turned right on 18ᵗʰ Street accordingly.

Parts of Speech: INTERJECTIONS   *Name* _____

An interjection is simply a word that expresses _____.

It is separated from the rest of the sentence by a _____ or an

_____ .

Examples: (The interjection is in bold type.)

Oh! There's a movie star!

Hah! That can't be true.

Oh, I love this song.

Ouch! That hurts!

Wow! You won first place!

Ah, I'm glad to sit down.

Practice: Write each interjection you find in the space after each sentence.

1. Wow! Look at that list of applicants! _____

2. So, how did you do on your test? _____

3. Well, I guess I'll go home before the next show. _____

4. Ew! That tastes terrible! _____

5. Oh yeah, I have to get my coat. _____

6. Hey! That was a great shot! _____

Practice: Finish each sentence below by writing an interjection on the blank line.

1. _____ ! Watch out!

2. _____ ! I think it's getting worse.

3. _____ ! They've landed!

4. _____ , maybe she changed her mind.

5. _____ , it probably won't matter anyway.

6. _____ ! Isn't that awful!

7. _____ , you don't really mean that, do you?

8. _____ ! Why did I do that?

Quiz   *Parts of Speech:* **NOUNS**   *Name* _____

A **noun** names a _____, _____, _____, or _____.

Directions: Underline all the nouns you can find in the following sentences. Be careful not to call a word a noun if it is not acting like a noun in the sentence.

1. The whole class left for the field trip.

2. Your happiness is my major concern.

3. Ten cards were sent to the sick children at Research Medical Center.

4. The mice scampered under the roll-top desk and around the floor boards.

5. The soldiers fought for freedom under General Hockaday.

6. Janice and Marlene tried to sneak into the theater.

7. List all the **proper nouns** you underlined in the above sentences:

_____

8. List all the **plural nouns** you underlined in the above sentences:

_____

Directions: Write an original sentence that includes at least one common noun and one proper noun. Make sure your sentence starts with a capital letter and ends with an end mark (period or question mark). It has to be a proper sentence. Write a "c" above your common noun and a "p" above your proper noun.

_____

_____

Directions: Fill in the missing items on the table below. Write the appropriate form of the noun under each column heading. The first one has been done for you as an example.

Singular Noun	Singular Possessive	Plural Form	Plural Possessive
goose	goose's	geese	geese's
lady			
dog			
girl			
key			
snake			
building			
flower			

Directions: Select one row of words. Write a sentence showing the appropriate use of each noun.

Example: goose   goose's   geese   geese's

1. The goose honked as it flew.
2. The goose's foot was injured.
3. The geese flew in formation.
4. The geese's flight was miles long.

1. _____

2. _____

3. _____

4. _____

Quiz *Parts of Speech: PRONOUNS* *Name* _____

A **pronoun** is a word that _____ _____ _____ of a noun.

The **antecedent of the pronoun** is the _____ to which the pronoun refers.

Directions: *Circle all the pronouns you can find in the following sentences.*

1. We were surprised that nothing went wrong.

2. Your happiness is my major concern.

3. He says he doesn't know why you called him.

4. This is the best gift you have ever given us.

5. My aunt wrapped the gift herself.

6. Please tell us whose name you wrote down.

7. The paper with no name is mine, not yours.

8. Those are the only forms that were turned in.

9. Many do not bend their knees when they shoot the ball.

10. He carried the boxes himself because his helpers did not arrive in time.

Directions: *Of the pronouns you circled in the sentences above, list as many as you can from each category below.*

Personal Pronouns	Indefinite Pronouns	Possessive Pronouns	Reflexive Pronouns	Demonstrative Pronouns

Quiz *Parts of Speech: ADJECTIVES*   *Name* _____

An **adjective** is a modifier. An **adjective** describes or gives more

information about a _____. An adjective will answer one of these

three questions:

    1. _____?   3. _____?

    2. _____?

Directions: *Underline all the adjectives you can find in the following sentences. Use the three questions above to identify the adjectives.*

1. The dented fender will cost you a little money.

2. We like the Cajun flavor in that soup.

3. Ten cards were sent to the sick children at the local hospital.

4. The tiny mice scampered under the roll-top desk and around the floorboards.

5. Mexican food is my favorite, especially spicy beef burritos.

6. Your sister is kind and courageous.

7. His room always looks neat and orderly.

8. A few kids stayed after school for more help.

9. She is the happiest child you've ever seen.

10. Our Oklahoma relatives will visit us next month.

Directions*: On the line below, write one original sentence that contains at least two adjectives. Circle the adjectives you used.*

_____

A verb names an _____ or expresses a state of _____.

A verb that names an action is called an _____ verb.

A verb that expresses a state of being is called a _____ verb.

Directions: In the sentences below, underline the simple subject once and the simple verb twice. In the blank, write an "A" if the verb is an action verb or "L" if the verb is a linking verb.

_____ 1. The meat spoiled.   _____ 6. Will you call me later today?

_____ 2. His car stalled in the intersection.   _____ 7. We are going with you.

_____ 3. The earth is round.   _____ 8. Her coat felt soft and warm.

_____ 4. The snake crawled out from below the rock.

_____ 5. The little girl felt the coat's soft collar.

Directions: For each of the sentences below, write *mv* above each main verb, and write *hv* above each helping verb.

1. The cake will have burned by then.

2. She must have left it alone for too long.

3. You may choose your elective classes.

4. Has she applied for a job yet?

5. Your teacher asked for your homework.

6. Can you give her a pencil?

Quiz *Parts of Speech: VERBS (2)*   *Name* _____

A verb names an _____ or expresses a state of _____.

A verb that names an action is called an _____ verb.

A verb that expresses a state of being is called a _____ verb.

The verb phrase consists of the main verb and any _____ verbs.

Directions: In the parentheses following each sentence, there is a present tense verb. Decide which form of the verb belongs in the context of the sentence and write that word in the blank. The first two sentences are done for you.

1. She ____**burst**____ into the room right after passing period. (burst)

2. The children have ____**broken**____ every piece of furniture. (break)

3. When the dog growled at him, the boy _____ it. (bite)

4. He _____ a pet snake for show-and-tell.   (bring)

5. The teachers have _____ to record their grades. (begin)

6. Everybody _____ from the fountain at recess yesterday. (drink)

Directions: Circle the verb that agrees with the subject in number (meaning, plural or singular) in Academic English.

1. She (sweep *or* sweeps) the driveway every Saturday.

2. The three friends (drive *or* drives) to school together.

3. We (think *or* thinks) they are just joking about leaving.

4. Fred (do or does) his chores quickly so he can play.

5. Daddy (sing *or* sings) while he works on the car engine.

Quiz *Parts of Speech:* ADVERBS

Name _____

An **adverb** is a modifier. An **adverb** describes or gives more information

about the _____, an _____, or another_____.

An adverb will answer one of these three questions:

1. _____? 2. _____?

3. _____? 4. _____ ?

Directions: *Underline the adverbs in each of the following sentences. The number following each sentence tells how many adverbs are in that sentence. Make sure the word you underline answers one of the four questions that adverbs answer.*

1. Babe Ruth's record was finally broken. (1)

2. John could barely hear Julie's voice. (1)

3. The crowd cheered wildly most of the time. (2)

4. Happily, the game is now played differently. (2)

Directions: Circle the correct adverb or adjective choice in the parentheses for each sentence.

1. Of the two workers, James works (*harder* or *hardest*).

2. Among the twenty students, Max runs (*faster* or *fastest*).

3. The youngest child seemed to be the (*happier* or *happiest*).

Directions: *Rewrite this sentence in Academic English (without double negatives):* **Don't nobody want to go to Texas with you.**

_____

Quiz *Parts of Speech:* **PREPOSITIONS**

Name _____

A **preposition** is a word that shows the relationship between a _____ or pronoun and some other word in the sentence.

A **prepositional phrase** consists of the _____, the _____ of the preposition, and all words between those two words.

When might the subject or the verb of a sentence be found in a prepositional phrase? _____

Directions: Enclose each prepositional phrase in parentheses.

1. We heard about the accident from Alex and Curtis.

2. Between you and me, he didn't even like her until last week.

3. Throughout the summer, we talked on the phone every day.

4. She announced his birthday over the intercom.

5. Your project is due by next Friday instead of next Wednesday.

6. We went into the House of Mirrors at the carnival.

7. He tried calling after 8:00 a.m. and before noon.

8. Without her best friend, she felt lonely and bored.

9. Beside his desk, in the aisle, sat his old backpack.

10. We rode our bikes over the highest hill and into the next county.

11. She chose the painting with the blue flowers in the white frame.

12. He wrote us concerning the petition for cleaner water.

13. Darrin and David drove the go-cart over their property before sunset.

Directions: Circle the correct form of the pronoun in each pair. Enclose the prepositional phrases in parentheses.

1. Let's sit between (she, her) and (he, him).

2. The librarian is talking about you and (I, me).

3. With (who, whom) did you skate last night, Karen?

4. Sandy built a wall of sand around Josh and (I, me).

5. The driver left without the coach and (they, them).

Directions: On the lines below, write eight sentences. Each sentence must be written correctly, with a capital letter to start and an end mark to stop. Each sentence must contain a prepositional phrase. You may not use the same preposition twice. When you have written your sentences, enclose your prepositional phrases in parentheses.

1. _____

2. _____

3. _____

4. _____

5. _____

6. _____

7. _____

8. _____

QUIZ: *Coordinating and Correlative Conjunctions*

Name _____

Directions: List the coordinating conjunctions:

1. _____ 2. _____ 3. _____

4. _____ 5. _____ 6. _____

7. _____

Directions: Fill in the missing words for the following correlative conjunctions:

    1. not only ... _____ _____   2. either ... _____

    3. _____ ... nor   4. both ... _____

    5. whether ... _____   6. not ... _____

Directions: Circle every conjunction you can find in the following sentences. Don't forget that correlative conjunctions are made up of more than one word.

1. Both the red letters and the green letters will look good on the board.

2. John, David and Mark all gave their reports today.

3. You may either take out the trash or wash the dishes.

4. Not only did he shovel the walk, he also salted the front porch.

5. We wanted to leave at 5:00, yet we still had a lot of work to do.

6. You turned your test in, but she didn't.

7. Whether we eat dinner or watch the movie first is up to you.

8. Neither the Chiefs nor the Raiders were in the play-offs.

QUIZ: *Subordinating Conjunctions* *Name* _____

Directions: Circle the subordinating conjunction in each sentence. Then, put brackets around the entire subordinate clause (the clause that goes with the subordinating conjunction). Finally, if the subordinate clause comes first in the sentence, make sure you put a comma right after the entire subordinate clause.

Examples: He dried the dog with a towel [(after) he bathed it.]

[(After) he bathed it,] he dried the dog with a towel.

1. Because we were undefeated everyone wanted to beat us.

2. I gave him a pass so that he could go to class without being tardy.

3. We take the mail inside when we go home.

4. As long as you call first you can come over this weekend.

5. Whatever you want to do for the talent show you need to show the sponsor.

6. Until we give you a number you must wait in line.

7. Mrs. Jones did not know when the event would start.

8. Though she practiced her performance wasn't very good.

9. Put your leg up on the chair if it hurts.

10. Now that we have finished watching our show you can turn the channel.

11. We heard that she was suspended for fighting.

12. He makes more money than you would believe.

QUIZ: *Conjunctive Adverbs*   *Name* _____

Directions: Circle the conjunctive adverb in each sentence. Put in the correct punctuation for each conjunctive adverb.

1. She wanted to check out one library book instead he had to get another.

2. Jeff was turned down for the job. This young man is determined nevertheless to get hired.

3. After working in the cold, Pete was too tired to eat. He did take a shower however.

4. John didn't know you called otherwise he would have called back.

5. We studied every day for 30 minutes for two weeks subsequently we got a good grade on the test.

6. He didn't know what had happened at the skating rink besides he didn't really care.

7. Ellen makes a speech to the committee three times a year still she gets nervous each time.

8. We planned to eat at McDonald's instead we ended up at Taco Bell.

9. She scored high on the ACT therefore she was offered several scholarships.

10. We waited for hours finally they came walking around the corner.

11. Joe likes antique cars similarly he's interested in vintage motorcycles.

12. We tried hard to follow the directions to the theater. We turned right on 18th Street accordingly.

Parts of Speech: COMPREHENSIVE REVIEW

Name _____

Directions: See if you can identify each and every word as a single part of speech. Use the abbreviations in the box below, and write the abbreviation for the part of speech above each word in the paragraph. Remember to ask yourself the questions necessary to identify certain parts of speech. The word's part of speech depends upon how it is being used in the sentence.

---

n = noun   **pro** = pronoun   **adj** = adjective   **v** = verb

adv = adverb   **conj** = conjunction   **prep** = preposition

int = interjection   **conj adv** = conjunctive adverb

Use **adj**. *for the articles: a, an, the*

Paragraph #1:

Our trip to Miami was amazing! The flight from Kansas City takes only three hours, so we got a nice nap in the air. When we landed, we picked up our luggage and found a shuttle bus to the hotel. The shuttle took almost an hour, but once we got to the Holiday Inn on Biscayne, we knew it was worth the wait. We quickly dropped off our bags in our hotel rooms and met again in the lobby. We walked to the outdoor shopping area across the street. Although the winter weather in K.C. brought freezing temperature and snow, the night air in Miami was 75 degrees!

Directions: Use the abbreviations in the box below, and write the abbreviation for the part of speech above each word in the paragraph.

```
n = noun      pro = pronoun      adj = adjective      v = verb

adv = adverb      conj = conjunction      prep = preposition

int = interjection      conj adv = conjunctive adverb

Use adj. for the articles: a, an, the
```

Paragraph #2:

      Panera Bread is a chain restaurant that specializes in pastry and coffee, sandwiches, salads, and soups. My favorite breakfast is a toasted cinnamon crunch bagel with honey walnut cream cheese. My sister likes the bacon, egg, and cheese bagel sandwich. We take our drinks with us as we walk around the shops at the mall.

Paragraph #3:

      When you first start middle school, you may struggle with the transition. While you had only one teacher in elementary school, you will have six different teachers in middle school. You will also have a locker. Obviously, there will be many more students at the middle school. Finally, you will have no recess!

Directions: Use the abbreviations in the box below, and write the abbreviation for the part of speech above each word in the paragraph.

---

n = noun   **pro** = pronoun   **adj** = adjective   **v** = verb

adv = adverb   **conj** = conjunction   **prep** = preposition

int = interjection   **conj adv** = conjunctive adverb

Use **adj**. *for the articles: a, an, the*

Paragraph #4:

Most of the students in my school participate in the Math Relays competition every year. At the school level, every student takes math tests during their math classes. Their scores are compared to those of other students throughout the district, and medals are awarded for first, second, and third places. On one Saturday, several relay teams from each school travel to Wyandotte High School. There, they compete in math contests for most of the day. Our school almost always ranks high at the end. The students wear their math relays t-shirts and their medals to school on the following Monday.

Converting Common Usage to Academic English

Name _____

Regional or Ethnic Dialect	Academic English Rule	Revised as Academic English
"That's mines." "Mines is red."	The pronoun "mine" (with no "s") is already possessive.	"That's mine." "Mine is red."
"They built it theirselves." "They better learn to do it theirselves."	"Theirselves" is not a word in Academic English.	"They built it themselves." They better learn to do it themselves."
"Them kids come late every day." "Get them shoes off the sofa."	"Them" is not a demonstrative pronoun in Academic English.	"Those kids come late every day." "Get those shoes off the sofa."
"I need a envelope for my letter." "I brought a apple for a snack."	Use "an" instead of "a" before a word that starts with a vowel (a, e, i, o, u).	"I need an envelope for my letter." "I brought an apple for a snack."
"We ain't doing no push ups." "Don't none of us have your money."	Academic English does not use double negatives. "Ain't" is seldom, if ever, used in Academic English.	"We aren't doing push ups." Or, "We won't do any push ups." "None of us have your money."
"She had went to the meeting." "He has went to the store."	Academic English does not use a helping verb with "went". Use "went" with no helping verb, or use "gone" with a helping verb.	"She went to the meeting." Or, "She had gone to the meeting." "He went to the store." Or, "He has gone to the store."

Practice Converting Common Usage to Academic English:

Rewrite each sentence according to the rules of Academic English.

1. Ain't nothing you can do about it.

_____

2. He had went to the church service.

_____

3. She gone already.

_____

4. Don't nobody know who borrowed her notebook.

_____

5. She chose a album for her friend.

_____

6. Them are the sweetest pears!

_____

7. Them seniors need to get theirselves together.

_____

8. Mines are the yellow ones.

_____

9. She picked up a umbrella on her way out.

_____

Appendix

Parts of Speech: Note-Taker – Teacher's Key

Answers to Comprehensive Review Paragraph (on page 80)

How to Use Your Knowledge of Parts of Speech to Improve Your Writing Today

Part of Speech	Definition or Job (how this part of speech works in a sentence)	Questions this part of speech answers, or list of examples	Tips and Clues
Noun	Names a person, place, thing, or idea. Works as the subject of the sentence. Works as an object (object of the preposition, direct object, indirect object) in the sentence.	Who? Whom? What?	Capitalize proper nouns. Do not capitalize common nouns.
Pronoun	Takes the place of a noun or a group of nouns. A pronoun works just like a noun.	List of examples: *he, she, it, her, him, they, them, us, we, everyone, someone, no one, nobody, anyone, this, that, those,* etc.	Sometimes this, that, these, those may be used to describe a noun; when they describe a noun, they are adjectives: Ex. *These* belong to me. (*These* is a pronoun.) Ex. *These* cards belong to me. (*These* is an adjective, modifying cards.)
Adjective	Modifies, describes, or gives more information about a noun or pronoun.	What kind? Which one? How many? How much?	
Verb	Names an action (such as *write, run, talk, work*) or a state of being (such as *am, is, are, was, were, be, being, been*). A verb that names an action is an *action verb*. A verb that names a state of being is a *linking verb*.	What did someone or something do? List of helping verbs: *has, had, have, will, did, do, can, could, should, might,* etc.	The verb of a sentence may be a verb phrase, consisting of the main verb plus any helping verbs. Ex. We *should have gone* to the movies. *Gone* is the main verb. *Should* and *have* are helping verbs. The entire verb phrase is *should have gone.*
Adverb	Modifies, describes, or gives more information about a verb, an adjective, or another adverb.	When? Where? How? To what extent?	Many words that end in –*ly* are adverbs, telling how the action of the verb is performed, such as *barely, sadly, loudly.* These words, are always adverbs: *rather, really, not, too, very, always.*

Part of Speech	Definition or Job (how this part of speech works in a sentence)	Questions this part of speech answers, or list of examples	Tips and Clues
Preposition	Shows the relationship between a noun or pronoun and some other word in the sentence. The prepositional phrase starts with the preposition and ends with a noun or pronoun, which is called the object of the preposition. The entire prepositional phrase acts as one part of speech, either an adjective or an adverb.	List of examples: *above, against, upon, over, below, beneath, under, on, up, down, for, to, of*, and many more. Ex. The book is *on* the desk. The preposition *on* answers the question, "Where is the book in relation to the desk?"	When analyzing a sentence, take out the prepositional phrases by enclosing them in parentheses and ignoring them. The subject of a sentence is NEVER in a prepositional phrase. The verb of a sentence is NEVER in a prepositional phrase.
Conjunction	A word, or a pair of words, that joins words or sentence parts. <u>Kinds of conjunctions:</u> Coordinating conjunctions Correlating conjunctions Subordinating conjunctions Conjunctive Adverbs	List of examples: *and, but, or, nor, for, so, yet, either/or, neither/nor, not only/but also, both/and, whether/or*	Some of the words used as conjunctions may also be used as other parts of speech. You have to determine how the word is being used in a particular sentence to know whether it is a conjunction or a preposition.
Interjection	A single word (or two) that expresses strong emotion. An interjection is usually written by itself, with a capital letter and an exclamation mark.	List of examples: *Wow!* *Awesome!* *Hey!* *Ridiculous!*	A single word (or two) that expresses strong emotion. An interjection is usually written by itself, with a capital letter and an exclamation mark.

Answers to Comprehensive Review Paragraph (on page 80)

pro n prep n v   adj   adj n   prep   n   n
Our trip to Miami was amazing! The flight from Kansas City

                 conj   conj
v   adv adj   n   adv pro v adj adj n prep adj n   adv   pro
takes only three hours, so we got a nice nap in the air. When we

v   pro v   adv pro   n   conj v adj adj n prep adj
landed, we picked up our luggage and found a shuttle bus to the

                                          conj
n   adj   n v   adv adj n conj adv pro v prep adj
hotel. The shuttle took almost an hour, but once we got to   the

      n   prep   n   pro v pro v adj adj n   pro adv
Holiday Inn on Biscayne, we knew it was worth the wait. We quickly

v   adv pro n prep pro adj   n   conj v adv prep adj n
dropped off our bags in   our hotel rooms and met again in   the lobby.

                                          conj
pro v   prep adj adj   adj   n   prep adj n   adv
We walked to   the outdoor shopping area across the street. Although

adj adj   n prep n v   adj   n   conj n
the winter weather in K.C. brought freezing temperatures and snow,

adj adj n prep   n v adj n
the night air in Miami was 75 degrees!

How to Use Your Knowledge About the Parts of Speech to Improve Your Writing Today

Two camps of educators hold very strong opinions about whether we should spend any class time on formal or traditional grammar lessons. Surely, students don't need to learn parts of speech, do they? How can the knowledge of parts of speech help our students improve their writing?

I believe that it can.

I agree with critics of isolated grammar instruction, that students will be more engaged in learning grammar structures when that learning is tied directly to their own efforts at writing. There are very easy ways to accomplish this.

After leading a lesson on any part of speech, ask students to underline, circle or highlight all of the nouns (or pronouns, or adjectives, or whatever part of speech you have been teaching) that they can find in their own draft. Ask them to notice *how* they used that particular part of speech. Just calling attention to one brick in the wall, so to speak, will focus the writer's attention on a word choice they might improve.

<u>As their writing coach, you might ask your students to make thoughtful decisions about the **nouns** they have used.</u> Would a proper noun (a more specific name) give more information about a character or a place than a common noun? "The boy" is much less descriptive than a thoughtfully selected name for a character, such as "Roger Dodger," "Bud," or "John-Boy."

If the writer uses a proper noun to name a building or a town, the reader is more likely to "see" that place in his or her imagination. Compare these two descriptions:

> *The girl rode her bike down the street to the library.*
> vs.
> *Kayla coasted on her Schwinn two-wheeler down Sandy Cove Lane to the Shoreline Public Library.*

Using proper nouns instead of common nouns adds quite a bit more detail so that the reader can imagine the scene. The writer creates more interest and appeal simply by changing common nouns to proper nouns, especially in narrative or fiction writing.

Can the student writer identify the antecedent of every **pronoun**? A common error writers make is to use a pronoun with no clear antecedent. For example, look at the pronoun "they" in this sentence:

We called the television station all day, but they did not answer.

In this sentence, the writer has used the pronoun "they" to refer to the television station; however, a television station cannot answer a phone. What the writer really means is that no one who works at the television station answered the phone; the people did not answer. To correct this sentence, he might write instead:

We called the television station all day, but nobody answered.

A faulty pronoun reference can result in a sentence of unclear meaning. For example, notice how the writer uses the pronouns "he" and "it" in the following sentence:

After John tossed the ball to his dog, he chewed it up.

As written, this sentence actually means that John chewed up the ball or John chewed up his dog. To fix this faulty pronoun reference, you could revise the sentence this way:

After John tossed the ball to his dog, his four-legged friend chewed it up.

Or, you could revise it even more simply, like this:

After John tossed the ball to his dog, the dog chewed up the ball.

Many writing experts dislike an overuse of adjectives. They assert that actions (verbs) convey images more effectively than lists of descriptors. The overuse of descriptors, **adverbs** or **adjectives**, sounds amateurish (even flowery) to seasoned readers and writers.

A look at his highlighted adjectives enables the young writer to analyze the effect of those adjectives on his overall composition. He or she may opt for one perfectly-chosen adjective rather than a list of trite descriptors. Maybe the student's draft has no descriptor, so the writer analyzes whether adding one or two will improve his or her composition, or not.

Focusing on verb selection for every sentence can improve a composition significantly. Verbs should be selected for connotation, as well as denotation, and for aptness, for perfect expression. Did that character "murmur", "croak", "spit", "whisper", or "sing" the words he spoke in the story?

Did that character "trudge", "skip", "float", or "stomp" away from her mother? You can capture a mood or create an image with the careful selection of a specific verb.

Examining the use of one part of speech at a time, experimenting with a thesaurus and various word choices, is a useful exercise as we learn to write.

The suggestions in this article for applying your knowledge about the parts of speech is common knowledge among writers and writing coaches. Why shouldn't we and our students learn these easily applied composition techniques as well, to improve our writing?

Your students will be surprised and delighted to see a difference between their first draft and their revised draft after they apply these simple changes in word choice, all based on their knowledge of the parts of the speech

www.ingramcontent.com/pod-product-compliance
Lightning Source LLC
LaVergne TN
LVHW081348060426
835508LV00017B/1467